3 0063 00001 0902

Apr10- DPBG

GREAT PETS

Lizards

Ruth Bjorklund

 **Marshall Cavendish**
Benchmark

New York

For Marion

Marshall Cavendish Benchmark
99 White Plains Road
Tarrytown, New York 10591
www.marshallcavendish.us

All Web sites were available and accurate when this book was sent to press.

Editor: Karen Ang
Publisher: Michelle Bisson
Art Director: Anahid Hamparian
Series Designer: Elynn Cohen

Library of Congress Cataloging-in-Publication Data

Bjorklund, Ruth.
Lizards / by Ruth Bjorklund.
p. cm. -- (Great pets)
Summary: "Describes the characteristics and behavior of pet lizards, also discussing their physical appearance and
place in history"--Provided by publisher.
Includes bibliographical references and index.
ISBN 978-0-7614-2997-5
1. Lizards as pets--Juvenile literature. I. Title. II. Series.

SF459.L5B56 2009
639.3'95--dc22
2008017560

Front cover: A green anole
Title page: An anole
Back cover: A chameleon

Photo research by Candlepants, Inc.
Front cover: Joyce & Frank Burek / Animals Animals

The photographs in this book are used by permission and through the courtesy of:
Shutterstock: Brian Dunne, 1; Nikita Tiunov, 14; Eric Isselee, 15; Lana Langlois, 22; Michael Ledray, 23(top); Michelle D.
Milliman, 25; Gina Smith, 34; bouzou, 36; Francois Etienne du Plessis, 39; Julie Keen, 42; Michelle Marsan, back cover.
Art Resource, NY: Werner Forman, 4; Private Collection, 7. The Bridgeman Art Library: Private Collection, Photo ©
Boltin Picture Library, 6. Animals Animals: Klaus Uhlenhut, 8; Joyce & Frank Burek, 10; Robert Lubeck, 17; Zigmund
Leszczynski, 26, 18; Joe Mc Donald, 31; Stephen Dalton, 40. Peter Arnold Inc.: John Cancalosi, 12; Biosphoto / Klein &
Hubert , 16; James Gerholdt, 21(lower); C. Steimer, 28, 32, 38, 41; Biosphoto / Labat & Rocher, 30; Peter Frischmuth,
44; P. Wegner , 45. Minden Pictures: Gerry Ellis, 20; Mary McDonald, 21(top). Photo Researchers Inc.: James H.
Robinson, 19, 43; Anthony Mercieca, 23(lower).

Printed in Malaysia
6 5 4 3 2 1

Contents

Chapter 1	**All about Lizards**	5
Chapter 2	**Types of Lizards**	13
Chapter 3	**Where to Find Your Pet Lizard**	25
Chapter 4	**Caring for Your Lizard**	33
Glossary		46
Find Out More		47
Index		48

1

All about Lizards

Lizards belong to a group of vertebrates (animals with backbones) called reptiles. Reptiles first appeared on Earth about 350 million years ago. They were the first animals to live nearly all of the time on land, rather than in water. There are more than 7,000 **species**, or types, of reptiles. Reptiles are divided into five groups and lizards are the largest group with more than 4,000 species. Lizard species can be native to deserts, prairies, forests, jungles, mountains, or even the ocean. They are found naturally everywhere in the world but Antarctica.

Like other reptiles, lizards are cold-blooded. The scientific term is **ectothermic**, which means that the animal cannot control its own body heat and must seek warmth from the sun. It also must find shade or water to cool down. All reptiles have dry, scaly skin. They breathe through lungs and

For thousands of years, lizards have played an important part in the mythology, religion, and culture of many different people. A lizard is part of the design on this African dance mask.

lay eggs or give birth to live young. All reptile young are fully developed when they are hatched or born and can live more or less independently.

Lizard Legends

Lizards can be found around the world, and stories have been told about them throughout time. The Aboriginal people in northern Australia believed in the thunder god *Ipilya*, who was a 100-foot-long giant gecko. He lived in swamps and drank nothing but mud and water. Afterward, he spit it all back into the sky to cause fierce rains and thunderstorms.

This lizard statue was made by people who lived in Central or South America several thousand years ago. The lizard was so respected, that this statue was made out of gold.

Another native Australian group believed that their lizard god created humans. He gave people a shape, and carved mouths, ears, and noses. Then he supplied them with tools such as a knife, spear, shield, fire, and the boomerang. In southern Africa, the San people of the Kalahari Desert (once called the Bushmen) also believed a lizard god created human beings.

In a legend from ancient Mexico, the lizard is a hero. One story tells of a time when the Sun disappeared. After it had been dark for many days, everyone became frightened. So all the animals set out to look for the missing Sun. They searched in lakes, rivers, forests and jungles, but could not find it. One by one everyone gave

Dragons—which have many lizard-like features— are often found in mythology and stories from around the world.

up searching, except for the lizard. Finally, the lizard found the Sun asleep under a rock. The lizard ran to tell the emperor. Together with a woodpecker, the emperor and lizard woke up the Sun and returned it to the sky.

CLEVER MOVES

In the wild, lizards have many enemies. To avoid being caught, they use some clever moves. Some pet lizards will do the same things.

- **Camouflage**. To escape their predator, many lizards blend into their surroundings by changing color or crouching to look like a twig or rock.
- **Illusion**. To trick their predators, some lizards have long wavy lines on their bodies and tails to make them seem like they are moving very, very fast.
- **Movement**. Many lizards run in a start-and-stop pattern which makes them hard to catch. They also move low to the ground and cast little or no shadow.
- **Hiding**. Some lizards hide under rocks or burrow into sand.
- **Deception**. Many lizards fool predators by seeming too nasty to eat, such as by having horns or spiky scales.
- **Bluffing**. Some lizards inflate their **dewlap** to appear larger and scarier.
- **Refuge**. Many lizards stay close to their homes, so that if they have to make a run for it, they do not have far to go. One lizard, the chuckwalla, wedges himself between rocks and puffs up its whole body so large that a predator cannot pull it loose.

When it feels scared, this frilled lizard sticks out the skin flaps on the sides of its neck so that it will look bigger.

Other cultures also respect and honor the lizard in their myths legends. In Hawaii, the god Mo'o was a water lizard who protec forgave their misdeeds, and healed their wounds. When people died, also guided human spirits to the afterworld. Along the Amazon River in South America, the Lizard God was lord of all the animals. In ancient China, the lizard-like dragon was one of the four holy animals on Earth. Dragons stood for wisdom, strength, and goodness. They also symbolized water and were thought to control the weather. The Japanese believed that their powerful Dragon King lived in the sea. He was thought to be strong, fair, and wise.

Real or imaginary, lizards are truly a wonder. For some of us, that makes them terrific pets.

Is a Lizard a Good Match For You?

Lizards make good pets because some types can be easy to care for and are very interesting to watch. With healthy food and proper care, a lizard can be a companion for many years. Lizards come in a range of colors, shapes, and sizes, each with their own special behaviors. Most lizards are quiet and they will not bother you with many demands. Though they do not like to be petted, many do not mind being handled.

Depending on the type you choose, pet lizards are not costly to care for or feed. Some lizard owners enjoy going outdoors to collect worms and insects to feed their pet. Others like raising food for their pet's dinner.

A lizard does not have fur, so you do not have to brush or comb it. Because it has no fur, people who get sick being near furry animals can safely care for a pet lizard. Though having a lizard is not for everybody, pet owners who like colorful, interesting, and unusual animals say a lizard is a great choice.

Before you bring your new lizard home, you must plan carefully. Some lizards are much easier to care for than others. **Veterinarians** (or "vets" for

Leopard geckos are excellent pets for first-time lizard keepers.

short), people who work in pet shops, and lizard experts and breeders will urge you to start out with an "easy" lizard, such as a leopard gecko, a green anole, or a blue-tongued skink. Once you are used to caring for an easy lizard, then you might keep another one that requires more care.

Choosing a lizard is not only about picking one because of its looks, size, or unusual behavior. You must know what your future pet will need and be able to have those supplies on hand. Some lizards eat plants, but most eat live insects, spiders, or worms. Some will eat baby mice or even chickens. Most need a variety of foods and vitamins.

Lizards are housed in a special cage, called a **terrarium**, and for small lizards, those usually do not take up a lot of space. The terrarium should be prepared before you bring your lizard home. Different types of lizards need different types of terrariums. Some need tall terrariums with branches to climb on. Others prefer shallow terrariums, with rocks to hide under. Some lizards need a pool of water to swim in, and others want hot, dry sand. Nearly all lizards must have special lighting to keep their bodies at a healthy temperature. This lighting can be very expensive. The terrariums also need ventilation (air flow) and shade.

Some types of lizards live a long time, maybe longer than you can imagine planning for. So it is very important to learn all you can about your future pet and its needs before it joins your family. But if you prepare well, your lizard will be happy and healthy and will entertain you daily with its clever and interesting habits.

2

Types of Lizards

Lizards have many special features. Unlike snakes, which are also reptiles, lizards have movable eyelids and a pair of ear openings. Lizards also have excellent vision. **Nocturnal** lizards—ones that are awake and hunt at night—such as most geckos, see very well in the dark. Lizards also have a good sense of smell. Many have an extra scent organ located in their mouth, called a Jacobsen's organ. They use their tongues to scoop up particles in the air and then press them against the roof of their mouths. The organ helps them smell their surroundings.

Some lizards have a flap of skin under the neck called a dewlap. To impress a female or frighten an enemy, lizards can inflate the dewlap to make themselves appear larger than they are. Others have **crests** on their heads, spines along their backs, and one— the Jackson's chameleon—has three horns on its head.

Some types of anoles make great pets. This green anole is a good choice because it does not grow too large.

Lizard Bodies

Most lizards are small animals with a thick, long body, and a long tapered tail. For some species, such as some skinks, the tail is actually an extra limb that helps it stay steady when walking or climbing. Most lizards have four

limbs with five clawed digits—or toes—on each foot. Some have fewer digits. Some are legless. The legless glass lizard, for example, is often mistaken for a snake. The glass lizard, like many other lizards, also has a fragile tail which easily breaks away when caught. Lizards that can shed their tails are usually able to grow new ones.

As they get bigger, all lizards shed the outer layer of their skin, which is called molting. The old skin peels off in pieces, revealing

This anole is shedding—or molting. After it is done molting, the white-colored dried up skin will fall off and the lizard will look like normal.

Some lizard scales are smooth, while others are rough. Lizard scales vary in size, shape, and color.

brighter new skin underneath. The scales of their skin are made of keratin, a horn-like substance. There are many types of scales, such as beaded, overlapping, rough, smooth, or spiny. Lizards often have more than one type of scales on their bodies.

Lizards come in a wide range of sizes, colors, and behaviors. There are numerous lizard families, or groups. Some of the main groups include geckos, iguanas, skinks, water dragons, and chameleons.

Geckos

Wild geckos live in the warmer regions of the world. Geckos are different from other lizards because they have special pads on their feet that allow them to walk on most dry surfaces. Their pads act like suction cups, and they can even walk upside down.

Geckos are insectivores, which means that they eat insects. Many geckos hunt for insects at night. The clever house gecko will wait beside a lit light bulb. When insects gather near the light, the gecko pounces and eats the bug. Other geckos are active during the day. Geckos can make some sounds. Owners especially love to listen to their pet gecko's chirps.

Tokay geckos may be really nice to look at and to listen to, but they can be very hard to handle. Only experienced lizard keepers should have this type of lizard.

One type of gecko is the Tokay gecko. This lizard is native to forests in Southeast Asia. As one of the largest geckos, the Tokay is about 14 inches long when full grown. Its skin is a beautiful light blue with pink or orange spots. At night, this gecko often makes sounds that are like barking. Some believe it sounds like it is calling out its name "to-keh." Tokay geckos do not like to be handled and can be very aggressive—or likely to bite. This type of gecko is not good for an inexperienced owner.

Leopard geckos, however, are very popular as pets. They are native to the dry, high plains of Afghanistan, Pakistan, and northern India. The skin of the leopard gecko looks much like its namesake, with black spots on a yellow

Leopard geckos come in a variety of colors and spots.

or brown background. The leopard gecko has bulgy eyes, movable eyelids, and a wide mouth that appears to be smiling. This gecko is very hardy, which makes it a popular pet. Taking care of a leopard gecko is not as hard as caring for other types of lizards. A leopard gecko loves a fresh bowl of water and a warm, sandy terrarium.

Iguanas

The iguana group has the largest number of lizards. Most are native to the Americas, from southern Canada to the tip of South America. Some wild iguanas live in trees and forests, while others are from the desert. One rare species—which is not kept as a pet—lives on the Galapagos Islands, which is off of the coast of Ecuador in South America. This marine iguana **basks** on the rocky beaches during the day. To eat, it dives down to the ocean floor to feed on seaweed.

Young green iguanas are popular pets because they start out so small. However, most people do not realize that these lizards can grow to be around four feet long and can weigh more than fifteen pounds.

Some popular pet iguanas are the green anole, the green iguana, the emerald swift, and the chuck-walla. Most iguanas have long bodies, dewlaps, and crests on their heads. Males are more brightly colored than females. Some iguanas, such as the green iguana and the chuckwalla are **herbivores**. This means that they eat only plants. Others, such as the green anole, eat insects.

Many of these lizards, such as the green iguana, start out as small babies, but grow to be very large adults. The green iguana, however, can grow to be more than 3 feet long, with a thick tail and sharp claws. As a young lizard, it needs a small terrarium, but full-grown iguanas need a lot of space. You must always consider how big the lizard will grow to be before buying or adopting one.

First-time lizard keepers who want to have an iguana may consider the green anole as a pet. The green anole is sometimes called the American chameleon, but it is not a true chameleon. When it is upset, some green anoles can change color from green to brown. Green anoles are small compared to other iguanas—these anoles grow to be about 8 inches long. A male green anole likes to show off. It has a pink dewlap below its neck, and when it wants to attract a female or tell another green anole to leave its territory, it blows up the dewlap. When it is angry, the male will also bob its head, puff up its throat and turn sideways. These actions make the anole seem large and threatening.

Some anoles will flash their dewlaps to attract a mate or to scare off other lizards.

Skinks

There are many types of skinks, though not all make good pets. Most skinks are shiny with smooth, overlapping scales. Their legs are short—sometimes you can barely see their legs. Skinks have pointed heads and very thick necks, making them look a little snake-like. Some skinks climb branches, but most prefer to scamper on leaves, twigs, and dirt. A few skinks will even burrow into the ground. Most skinks are insectivores and some are **carnivores**, which means that they are animals that eat mostly meat. Skinks are generally very shy so their terrariums should have hiding places.

The blue-tongued skink is often kept as a pet. It has a long thick body, short legs, and a big head. It can be quite large—around 20 inches. The blue-tongued skink is an

Blue-tongued skinks really do have blue tongues. They are popular pets because of this feature, but also because they are not too hard to handle and care for.

easy-to-care-for lizard, but it does need a large cage with many hiding places and a bowl of water big enough to bathe in. Its favorite foods are snails, earthworms, bananas, and some types of dog food.

Dragons

Some lizards are called dragons, though they do not all belong to the same species. The water dragon is sometimes known as the Chinese water dragon. These lizards grow to be very long— some more than 2 feet long! They require a very large terrarium with a pool of water. Water dragons are not good pets for first-time lizard owners because they require a lot of care.

Water dragons need a lot of room in their terrarium and require more care than other lizards.

The bearded dragon is a native of the rocky, dry regions of eastern Australia. Full grown, it is about 18 inches long and gray and brown. The bearded dragon has a line of spines along its neck and when alarmed, it puffs them up to appear dangerous. Many bearded dragons that are kept as pets are rather tame. They do not mind being gently handled. Some bearded dragons could be good pets for first-time lizard owners.

A bearded dragon flashes its "beard" of scales to scare off bigger animals or other lizards.

Chameleons

In the wild, chameleons live in trees. They move slowly, but their long, sticky tongues dart out quickly to snag insects. When a chameleon's mood or body temperature changes, the animal's skin changes color. Depending upon the type of chameleon, the skin can be red, brown, green, yellow, black, blue, white, or a combination of these colors. When certain types of chameleons are at rest for example, they may be green. When angry, they may turn yellow. Chameleons also change color so that they blend in with their surroundings.

There are several different types of chameleons. Different types have different features. For example, the Jackson's chameleon has horns on its head,

Like all chameleons, this panther chameleon moves very slowly, moving one foot at a time.

Caring for chameleons requires more work than other lizards like anoles or skinks.

while the panther chameleon and veiled chameleon do not. All chameleons have eyes that bulge. They can move their eyes in separate directions at the same time. This allows the chameleon to see what is in front and behind it without ever turning its head. Chameleons are extremely interesting lizards, but they are hard to take care of as pets.

Always do your research before you pick a type of lizard as a pet. Picking the right type can help to make sure you and your lizard are happy.

THE PLUMED BASILISK

Even though they look really neat, some lizards should not be kept by owners who are just starting out with lizards. The plumed basilisk is one of these lizards. It is a very aggressive lizard, but it is highly prized among experienced lizard keepers. One reason is because it looks like a dinosaur, with bright green scales, a double crest on its head and spines along its back. Plumed basilisks can grow to be about 2 feet long and are very fast runners. Some types of basilisks move so quickly that they can even run on the surface of a pool of water.

3

Where to Find
Your Pet Lizard

Most people buy lizards from a pet shop, reptile show, or a breeder. To find someone with a lizard for sale, try looking on the Internet or in magazines about pet reptiles. You can also contact a local veterinarian for suggestions. You may also ask about local reptile breeders or reptile societies.

Some reptile shows may be held near you. These shows are a good opportunity to visit with many reptile breeders and people who sell reptile supplies. The breeders will bring reptiles and supplies that they are selling. You do not have to buy from the breeders at the show, but it is a good way to look around at the different types of pet lizards. You can ask a lot of questions and see how big the different lizards grow to be, and what kind of supplies they will need.

You should never take or catch your lizard from the wild. Lizard breeders often have a large selection of lizards from which you can choose.

It is important that the person selling you a lizard knows exactly where the lizard came from. Lizards sold as pets can be wild caught, which means that they were captured in their native wild **habitat**. Lizards that are captive born, are animals born in **captivity** to wild-caught parents. Captive-bred lizards are born in captivity to parents that were also raised in captivity. People who care about animals will tell you not to buy a wild caught or

You should only buy or adopt a lizard that was born in captivity from parents that were also born in captivity. This adult leopard gecko and its baby are captive-bred lizards.

captive-born lizard. Captive-bred lizards are healthier and make better pets. Wild-caught and captive-born lizards are often treated poorly. They carry more disease and become stressed and weak when brought into captivity. Additionally, these lizards have been taken away from the natural wild habitat they were born in. Scientists worry about the shrinking numbers of lizards left living in the wild.

It is a good idea to visit more than one pet store or breeder and look at many lizards. Lizards can live a long time, so choosing the right one is an important decision. Choose the healthiest lizard you find. Do not think that you will be able to save or rescue a sick or weak lizard. Leave that to more experienced lizard owners.

Some lizard or reptile rescue societies have healthy lizards looking for good homes. These lizards are usually given to the rescue groups when their owners can no longer care for them. Members of the rescue group will most likely talk to you and find out what kind of lizard you want or are capable of keeping. Veterinarians or animal welfare societies often have information about local reptile rescue groups. You can also find the information on the Internet.

HERPETOLOGY

Herpetology is the scientific term for the study of reptiles and amphibians. The word comes from the Greek word *herpeton*, which means "things that creep and crawl on their bellies." Many lizard owners belong to Herpetological societies, or "Herp" societies, for short.

What to Look for

Wherever you get your lizard, you want to make sure you are going to bring home a healthy pet. Remembering these questions and points will help you when you pick out your lizard.

The Surroundings

Take note of the place where you are purchasing or adopting your lizard. Does the terrarium where the lizards are kept look clean? Terrariums with a

When you buy a lizard from a breeder or from a pet store, you must make sure that the terrarium they are kept in is not too crowded. Lizards kept in crowded terrariums are often unhealthy and do not usually make good pets.

lot of animal waste or old food will most likely house sick lizards. Do the lizards have enough space in their terrariums? Are several lizards cramped together in a small space? Responsible breeders and good pet stores will provide their lizards with a healthy environment.

How you feel about the breeder, the rescue group, or the people working at the pet store is also important. Do they seem to know a lot about lizards? Do not be afraid to ask the breeder or the rescue group how long they have been selling or adopting out lizards. The more experience a breeder or seller has, the more likely it will be that the lizards will be healthy. Can the people working at the pet store answer your questions? If they do not know a lot about taking care of lizards, it is likely that the lizards at the store are not well cared for. The lizards might be mistreated or unhealthy.

The Lizards

The store and terrariums may look good, but that does not matter if the lizards are unhealthy. Before you purchase or adopt a lizard, you must give it a thorough inspection.

Does the lizard's skin look clean? The scales should be free from sores, cuts, scratches, lumps, or bites from other lizards. Does the lizard have any small bugs crawling on it? These bugs, called mites, are a bad sign. You do not want to purchase or adopt a lizard that has these mites. The bugs can cause and spread disease and illness.

Are the lizard's eyes clear and bright? Cloudy eyes or a lot of watering or discharge from the eyes could be a sign of illness. Have the pet store worker

A lizard's eyes and nose should be clean and clear, without a lot of fluid or crusty build up.

or the breeder open up the lizard's mouth for you. Is the inside a healthy pink color? Problems with the lizard's mouth could mean that it will not eat properly and will get sick.

Watch the lizard in its terrarium. Does it breathe easily? Does it move around a lot? Does it look comfortable in its terrarium? Is the lizard alert and interested in you and its surroundings? Lizards that spend all their time staying still and not moving may be ill.

Ask to hold the lizard. This is important because you will be responsible for caring for the lizard and handling it when necessary. Do the lizard's

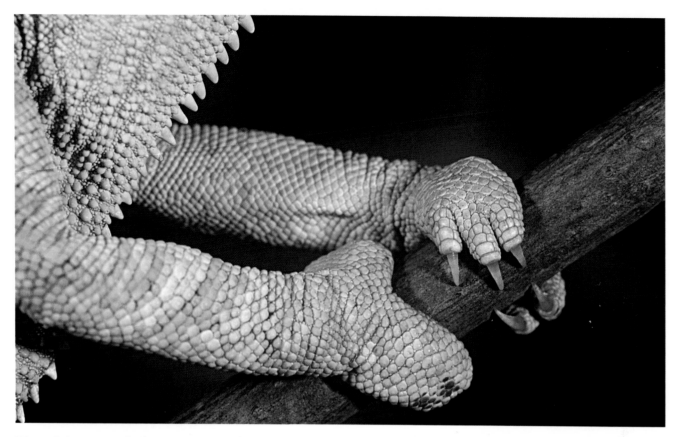

Lizards' toes and claws are very fragile and can be damaged easily. Before bringing home a lizard, make sure that its feet are free of injuries or infections.

muscles feel firm and strong? A very bony or very skinny lizard may be sick. When you hold the lizard does it pull away—which is a healthy, natural reaction—or does it act tired and weak? Does the lizard try to bite a lot? Most lizards will be nervous—and may try to bite—when they are passed from person to person. This is normal, but if a lizard struggles too much and cannot be held or removed from its cage, you may have problems taking care of it.

4

Caring for
Your Lizard

Your lizard's house will depend on the type of lizard you bring home. You should have the terrarium set up before you bring the lizard home. This way the lizard can get used to its new home as soon as you get it. Though each terrarium will be different, all must

- be escape-proof
- be big enough for the lizard
- be easy to clean
- have a heating system
- have proper lighting
- have good air flow or circulation
- have a way to control **humidity**, or how much moisture is in the terrarium's air.

Caring for a lizard does not have to be too hard. Being well informed and doing the necessary things for your lizard can help ensure a long and happy relationship between you and your pet.

Terrariums can be made from a combination of glass, wood, plastic, or metal. The terrarium should have openings for fresh air to flow. Cover the openings with wire mesh so that your lizard cannot escape. Pet stores often sell wire mesh covers for glass pet containers like fish tanks.

The floor of the terrarium will depend on the type of lizard. Desert-type or burrowing lizards like coarse sand. (Fine sand can get stuck in a lizard's scales). Woodland lizards like to walk on a mixture of sand, wood chips, and

Whether you use woodchips, soil, sand, gravel, newspapers, or a combination of any of these materials, you must always prevent waste from building up on the terrarium floor.

soil. Some lizards do not mind shredded newspapers. Large lizards do best with small stones or gravel. Remember that you want to be able to easily scoop up your pet's droppings and replace the flooring often with new, clean material. Arboreal lizards (lizards that live in trees) will need climbing branches and a tall terrarium. Though you may like having plants in a terrarium, your lizard might eat them. Some plants can be poisonous to lizards, so do your research before putting any live plant material inside. Plants can also add too much moisture inside the terrarium. Many lizard owners use plastic plants, or none at all. Plastic plants do not die, are hard for the lizards to eat, and can be cleaned when they are dirty. Most lizards like rocks or other features to climb on or hide behind.

Heating, humidity, and lighting are all very important parts of your terrarium. Lizards bask in sunlight to stay warm. Usually, natural sunlight shining through a

WARNING!

Lizards need the right amount of heat and light or they will become sick and die. The best way to provide these necessary things for your lizard is by using special heat lamps or heated rocks. However, these lamps and heated rocks need electricity to work. This means that they must be safely plugged into electrical outlets that can handle the energy needed for the light and heat. Heaters and lights can also become very hot and cause fires if they are not carefully positioned. When setting up a terrarium, have an adult help you decide where and how to safely place the lights and heating elements your lizard needs. Not only will your lizard be more comfortable in its terrarium, but your home will be safer.

Large lizards—like this green iguana—need a lot of space and big branches and rocks to rest upon. As your lizard grows, you might need to buy new supplies and a bigger terrarium. You should keep this in mind when you select the kind of lizard you want as a pet.

glass terrarium will be too hot for your lizard. So you must use special terrarium lights that imitate sunlight. Some people use "hot rocks," which are artificial rocks that have heaters in them. You should also supply your lizard with an unlit or shady area where it can cool off. Lizard species from jungles or tropical places or aquatic lizards (lizards that live by water) will need more humidity. Placing a special heater—made especially for reptile terrariums—in a pan of water can provide warmth and humidity for your lizard. There are many types of lights and each lizard requires a certain temperature range.

Your lizard's terrarium must be kept clean. Any water in the terrarium should be changed often. Lizard dropping should also be removed daily. At least once a month, place your lizard in a temporary box or container and take everything out of the terrarium. Have an adult help you wash and scrub the terrarium with a solution of soap, hot water, and diluted bleach (bleach that has a lot of water added to it). Make sure you rinse everything very well. Leftover soap or bleach can poison your lizard. Scrub or replace any decorations and put down new flooring material.

Most reptiles like lizards carry small bacteria called *Salmonella*. This bacteria can make you very sick. Whenever you handle your lizard or any part of its terrarium, be sure to wash your hands very well with an antibacterial soap. After cleaning its terrarium and decorations, be sure to have an adult disinfect the sink or tub you used. Never clean your lizard's terrarium in the kitchen or bathroom sink where you prepare food or brush your teeth. Do not kiss your lizard or put it on your face. The *Salmonella* germs can get into your mouth and make you sick. Your lizard could also bite and scratch you.

Feeding Your Lizard

You must be careful about what you feed your pet. A lizard is a wild animal, even if it is captive bred. Their bodies are used to a diet based on foods they would eat in their natural habitat. Lizards belong to one of four groups: herbivores, insectivores, carnivores, and omnivores. An iguana, for example is an herbivore. An iguana needs a carefully planned and balanced diet

If you give your lizard fresh fruits and vegetables, always be sure to remove the leftovers before they turn bad. Your lizard can get sick from eating spoiled food.

based on plants. You should feed an herbivore a variety of fruits, vegetables, leafy greens, and some grain. Good vegetables are snow peas, green beans, green peppers, and radishes. Collard greens, mustard greens, dandelion greens, and parsley are all leafy plants that will suit your pet. Fruits such as raspberries, figs, and pears will help round out a complete diet for your lizard. Be aware that some fruits and vegetables are not good for your lizard, such as spinach, rhubarb, carrots, bananas, and grapes. A veterinarian can tell you which fruits and vegetables are dangerous for your lizard.

Some lizards are insectivores, which means they hunt and eat insects like crickets. Pet stores sell live crickets for pet food. You may also catch crickets and other insects to feed your pet, but be sure to avoid poisonous insects, such as fireflies, or insects that might have eaten plants sprayed with pesticides— chemicals sprayed on crops to kill bugs. You will frighten your lizard if you feed it an insect that is too large. A handy rule is never feed your lizard an insect that is larger than two-thirds the size of the lizard's head. When you feed your lizard insects, drop the insects in the terrarium in different locations so that your lizard will hunt it down like it would in the wild. If there are insects left after your lizard has eaten, remove them or provide food for them. If the insects become hungry, they might

Mealworms are excellent sources of meat for insectivores and other meat-eating lizards.

attack your pet. Insectivores such as glass lizards and skinks also like to eat beetles, mealworms, waxworms, and earthworms.

A few lizards eat larger food. Some of the larger tegus, agamids, and monitors will eat baby mice, birds, eggs, and baby chickens. Most pet

A chameleon uses its long sticky tongue to catch a cricket.

owners buy frozen animals for their lizard's food. Meat-eating lizards should eat the whole animal. They benefit from the muscle meat and fat of the animal. Meat-eating lizards also get nutrition from the bones, fur, teeth, blood, and plant material in the animal's stomach. Large lizards that eat these big animals are not a good choice for the first-time lizard owner.

Most lizards are omnivores, which means that they eat a combination of foods. Omnivores like fruits and vegetables, leafy greens, insects, worms, and some meat. You may also feed them high-quality, low fat, canned cat or dog food. Many pet stores sell canned reptile food and reptile food pellets. Because your lizard is living in captivity, it will not always have the full diet it would in the wild. To fill out your lizard's diet, give your pet extra vitamins and minerals that are specially made for reptiles.

Every lizard needs water, but not every lizard needs it in the same way. Some lizards need a lot of water and may even want to swim in it. For

Ask a lizard expert, breeder, or veterinarian about how to give your lizard water. If you need to give your lizard a bowl or dish of water, be sure that it is not so deep that the lizard can crawl in and drown.

them, you should set out a pan of water. Other lizards only drink water by licking moisture off of leaves. For those lizards, you can use a spray bottle and cover leaves in the terrarium with a mist. To keep your pet healthy, be sure that the water is always fresh and clean.

Because every type of lizard needs special attention, it is very important to know what your particular lizard needs. You can find this information by contacting a veterinarian or lizard or herp specialist, asking a local pet store, reading about lizard care in books or online.

Health Care

Lizards are generally shy and do not like big changes. Changes in temperature, surroundings, or food will make your lizard feel stressed. When your lizard is stressed, it cannot fight disease. Keeping your pet clean, warm, and

If a lizard is very sick it may need special medication that only a veterinarian can give.

well-fed will help your lizard live a healthy life. If your pet seems sick, you should call a veterinarian. Not every veterinarian knows about caring for a lizard, but he or she will either help you or give you the name of someone who can.

One of the most common health problems for lizards is parasites, such as ticks or mites. These are tiny creatures that latch onto the skin of your pet. If your lizard has a tick, you may want to ask a veterinarian to show you how to carefully remove it. (With practice, you can most likely do this yourself.) The tick should be dabbed with rubbing alcohol and pulled away slowly and carefully. Pulling too hard or too quickly can hurt the lizard and leave parts of the tick inside its body. Mites are tinier creatures but can be more harmful. They are hard to spot on your pet or in your pet's terrarium until they multiply into large numbers. Mites show up as small spots that can be black, brown, or red. There are chemicals and medicines that can rid your terrarium of mites. Consult your vet or an experienced lizard owner for the best treatment.

You should also call your vet if your lizard is stressed, if it acts tired and does not eat well, or if you see changes in its color or lumps on its skin. These can be signs of other illnesses, such as breathing problems, skin problems, infections, or parasites that live inside the lizard's body, such as certain types of worms. Your vet should be able to give your pet medication and have some helpful advice for home care and disease prevention.

How to Handle Your Lizard

Most lizards do not like to be picked up a lot. But in order to care for your pet, you must be able to handle it safely. Always have an adult help you when you handle your lizard. If you are uncomfortable handling your lizard at first, do not be afraid to ask a breeder, a vet, or someone at a pet store to show you the proper way to hold your lizard.

First of all, never pick up your lizard by the tail because it could snap off. If you have a small

This anole has had its tail broken off. Some lizards can slowly grow back their tails, but others cannot. Never pick up a lizard by its tail. You could hurt the lizard and you could get bitten or scratched.

Larger lizards that are hard to hold should only be handled by adults or experienced lizard keepers.

lizard—up to 8 inches long—use your thumb and pointer finger and gently, but firmly, grasp the back of your lizard's head. Lightly gather the lizard's body with your other hand. It may squirm and try to bite you, but stay calm. If your lizard startles you, be very careful not to drop it. If you cannot get a good grip on the lizard, gently put it back into its terrarium, wait for a little while until it calms down, and then try again.

If your lizard is a medium size, or about 8 to 20 inches long, use one hand to grasp your lizard firmly around its chest. Use your thumb and pointer finger to control its head and prevent it from turning around. With your other hand, hold the lizard's hips and legs. Some medium-sized lizards can nip and are strong enough to break the skin when they bite. To prevent getting bitten, owners of medium or large lizards often wear leather gloves.

This bearded dragon is comfortable sitting in the hands of its owner. With practice, patience, and a lot of understanding, you and your lizard can become great friends.

If you have a large lizard more than 20 inches long you should not try to hold it by yourself. An adult should do the handling. He or she must wear leather gloves and clothes that are thick. Not only can a large lizard bite, but if it gets upset, it can make deep and painful scratches with its powerful claws. With one hand, the handler should grasp the lizard firmly around its neck. The other hand should hold the lizard's waist. The handler should gently but firmly use his or her elbow to press the lizard's rear legs and tail against the person's body.

Many lizard owners believe that the more you handle your pet, the tamer your pet will become. But others believe that lizards should be handled as little as possible, to keep them from becoming stressed. It will be up to you and your pet to decide what works best.

Lizards are some of the most fascinating creatures in the world. If you are lucky enough to have a pet lizard, you will have the chance to watch a truly wild creature in action every day. Take good care of your lizard and you will be rewarded with countless hours of interesting and entertaining companionship.

Glossary

bask—To lay in the sun or on a heated surface

captivity—Not living in the wild.

carnivore—An animal that eats meat.

crest—A decorative ridge of skin or spikes that may occur on the neck, back, and or tail.

dewlap—The flap of skin on the throat of some lizards.

ectothermic—A cold-blooded animal that cannot regulate its own body temperature and uses sunlight, shade and/or water to maintain a healthy body temperature.

habitat—The place where an organism lives

herbivore—An animal that eats plants.

herpetology—The study of reptiles and amphibians.

humidity—The amount of moisture found in the air.

nocturnal—An animal that is active at night.

omnivore—An animal that eats a combination of plants and meat.

Salmonella—Bacteria that can infect humans and cause stomach pain, vomiting, diarrhea, headache, fever, and chills.

species—Types of animals or plants which are closely related.

terrarium—The cage or container for housing an animal, such as a reptile.

veterinarian—A doctors who treat animals. A veterinarian is also called a "vet" for short.

Find Out More

Books

Bartlett, Richard D. *Anoles: A Reptile Keeper's Guide.* Hauppauge, NY: Barron's Educational Series, 2001.

Mattern, Joanne. *Lizards.* New York: Benchmark Books, 2002.

Heathcote, Peter. *Lizards.* Chicago: Heinemann Library, 2004.

Waters, Jo. *The Wild Side of Pet Lizards.* Chicago: Raintree, 2005.

Web Sites

The Green Iguana Society: Kids' Club
http://www.greenigsociety.org/kidsclub.htm

Lizards & Snakes: Alive!
http://www.amnh.org/lizards

Pet University: Reptiles
http://www.petuniversity.com/reptiles/lizards

San Diego Zoo
http://www.sandiegozoo.org/animalbytes/t-lizard.html

Index

Page numbers for illustrations are in **bold.**

adoption, 27
anoles, **1**, **12**, **14**, 19, **19**

babies, 19, **24**
basilisk, 23, **23**
breeders, 25
breeds, 16–23

cage *See* terrarium
camouflage, 8, 22
captivity, 26–27, 40
carnivore, 20, 39–40
chameleons, 15, 19, 22–23, **22**, **23**, 40
claws, 19, **31**, 45
cleaning, 37
cold-blooded (ectothermic), 5
color, 9, 11, 15, **15**, 18–19, 20, 22

dewlap, 13, 19, **19**
dragons, 21, **21**
      bearded, 21, **21**, **28**, **32**
      water, 15, 21

feeding, 9, 11, 17, 37–40, **38**, **39**, **40**
See also carnivore, herbivore, insectivore

geckos, 16–17, **16**, **17**,
      leopard, **10**, 17, **17**
      tokay, **16**, 17

handling (lizards), 9, 20, 30–31, 43–45, **43**, **44**, **45**

heat, 5, 11, 33, 35–36
health, 27, 28, 29, 30, 41–43, **42**
herbivore, 18
herpetology, 27
history, 5–9

iguana, 15, 18–19, **18**, **34**, **36**
illness, 28–29, 42–43, **42**
insectivore, 16, 20, 39, **39**, **40**

lighting, 11, 33, 35–36

molting, 14, **14**
mythology, 5–9

petting, 9, 43–45

reptile shows, 25

scales, 8, 13, 14–15, **14**, **15**, 20, 23, 29
size, 9, 11, 15, 18–19, 20, 23, 36, **36**, 43–45
skin, 14–15, **14–15**
skinks, 15, 20
      blue-tongued, 20, **20**

terrarium, 11, 17, 19, 20, 28–29, **28**, 33–37

veterinarian, 11, 25, 38, 41, 41–43, **42**

water, 11, 36, 37, 40–41, **41**
Web sites, 47

About the Author

Ruth Bjorklund lives on Bainbridge Island, across Puget Sound from Seattle, Washington, with her husband, two children, and five pets. She has written numerous books for young people. She was thrilled to explore the amazing world of lizards while writing this book.